Reading Essentials®
in Science

DIVERSE POPULATIONS

Bacteria and Viruses

MICHAEL CRUMPTON

PERFECTION LEARNING®

Editorial Director: Susan C. Thies
Editor: Mary L. Bush
Design Director: Randy Messer
Book Design: Emily J. Greazel
Cover Design: Michael A. Aspengren

A special thanks to the following for his scientific review of the book:
Paul Pistek, Instructor of Biological Sciences, North Iowa Area Community College

Image credits

©Mediscan/CORBIS: p. 5 (right); ©Lester V. Bergman/CORBIS: pp. 5 (bottom), 8 (bottom); ©Charles O'Rear/CORBIS: p. 8 (top); ©Bettman/CORBIS: p. 21; ©CORBIS: p. 22; ©Ted Spiegel/CORBIS: p. 35

AgeFoto: p. 34 (center); BananaStock Royalty-Free: p. 32; Center for Disease Control: p. 7; ClipArt.com: pp. 16, 30 (top); CORBIS Royalty-Free: p. 14 (top); Creatas Royalty-Free: p. 4; InsideOutPix Royalty-Free: pp. 3 (center), 12–13; iStock International: cover, pp. 1, 3 (top, bottom), 6, 10–11, 12, 13, 17, 23, 24, 25, 26, 28, 28–29, 29, 30 (bottom), 31, 33, 36, 37, 38, 39 (bottom); OAR/ National Undersea Research Program (NURP)/NOAA: p. 15; Perfection Learning/Michael A. Aspengren: pp. 9, 10, 11 (bottom), 14 (bottom), 18, 19, 20, 39 (top); Photos.com: p. 34 (top)

For information, contact

Perfection Learning® Corporation
1000 North Second Avenue, P.O. Box 500
Logan, Iowa 51546-0500.
Phone: 1-800-831-4190
Fax: 1-800-543-2745
perfectionlearning.com

1 2 3 4 5 6 PP 11 10 09 08 07 06

PB ISBN 0-7891-6986-x
RLB ISBN 0-7569-6386-9

Contents

chapter 1

Invasion!

You wake up with a sore throat and figure you must be getting a cold. After two days, however, your throat still hurts and no other signs of a cold have appeared. On the third day, your mom insists on taking you to the doctor to get it checked out.

The doctor feels your neck and peers down your throat with a small flashlight. "You definitely have an infection," she says, "but I can't tell what's causing it from just looking. It could be bacteria or a virus. We'll have to do some tests so we know how to treat it."

The doctor swabs your throat and sends the sample off to the lab. She promises to call as soon as the results are back.

Lots of things can cause a sore throat, but two of the most common causes are **bacteria** and **viruses**. These tiny invaders surround you all the time. Billions of them live inside you. Most of them are not harmful or even noticeable. However, a few, such as those that cause sore throats, can cause illnesses or diseases.

"It's strep throat," the doctor tells you when the results of your tests arrive. "It's caused by a bacteria called *Streptococcus pyogenes*. Since it's a bacterial infection, I can prescribe an **antibiotic** for it. The medicine should eliminate most of your symptoms within a day or two."

Streptococci bacteria

Bacteria from a throat culture (sample) growing in a petri dish

5

After the doctor hangs up, you think about what she said. What if it had been a virus making your throat sore? Would medicine have helped that too? And what are these bacteria that are running around in your body making you sick? You've heard the words *bacteria* and *virus* many times, but you've never really thought about what they were, where they come from, or how they make you sick. Maybe it's time to find out more about these bacterial and viral invaders.

chapter 2

Bacteria Basics

Bacteria are the most successful organisms on Earth. They have existed for more than 3 billion years. There are more bacteria in the world than all other organisms. In fact, if you put all of the bacteria in the world on one side of a seesaw and all of the other living things in the world on the other side, the bacteria would tip the seesaw downward.

Many bacteria live in groups called *colonies*. Colonies multiply quickly when food and temperature conditions are favorable. Each type of bacteria creates a unique colony formation. The sample of bacteria from your throat was allowed to multiply into a colony in the lab. This helped to identify what kind of bacteria it was.

Individual ID

One of the members in a colony of bacteria is called a *bacterium*.

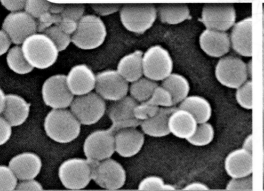

Staphylococcus aureus bacteria colony

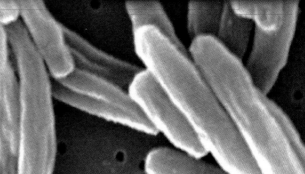

Mycobacterium tuberculosis bacteria colony

Sizing Up Bacteria

Bacteria come in a large range of sizes, but even the biggest are very small. The largest bacterium that has been discovered is about the size of the period at the end of this sentence. On the other hand, the smallest bacterium is so tiny that you would have to line up about 500 of them to be as wide as a human hair.

Many *Epulopiscium fishelsoni* bacteria can fit on the head of a pin. These are the largest bacteria known to exist.

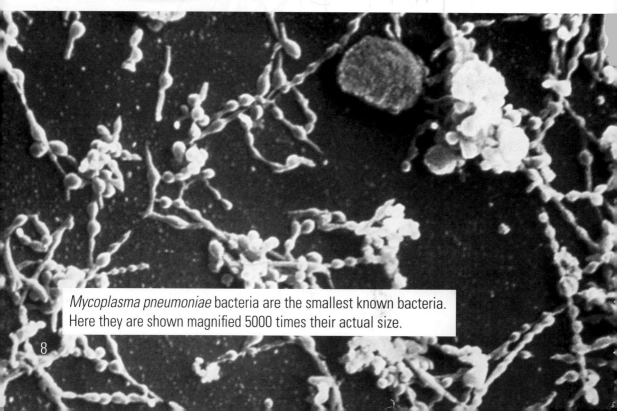

Mycoplasma pneumoniae bacteria are the smallest known bacteria. Here they are shown magnified 5000 times their actual size.

You're My Type

Thousands of bacteria have been identified and named. These bacteria come in a variety of shapes, but most fall into one of three categories.

Coccus are spherical or egg-shaped bacteria. Some types of coccus grow together in pairs, chains, or clumps. The streptococci bacteria that cause strep throat, for example, are spherical and form a chain like a string of pearls.

Bacillus bacteria are generally rod-shaped like a pill capsule. Some rod-shaped bacteria can be tapered, oval, or even curved. The deadly anthrax disease is caused by rod-shaped bacteria (*Bacillus anthracis*) that grow in lines like long trains.

Bacteria that look like spirals, corkscrews, or curvy waves are known as spirillum. *Helicobacter pylorus* is a spirillum bacterium that lives in people's stomachs and causes ulcers and digestive problems. It looks like a wavy earthworm.

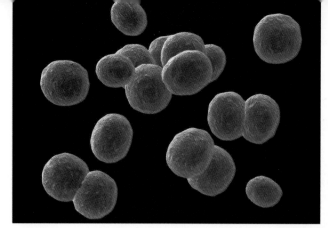

Coccus

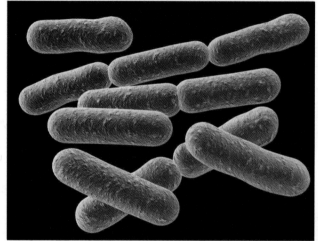

Bacillus

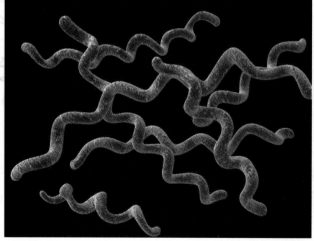

Spirillum

Singles Only!

Bacteria are single-celled organisms. This means their bodies consist of just one cell. All of the structures that a bacterium needs to live and grow are housed inside its single cell.

Most bacteria have a **cell membrane** surrounded by a **cell wall**. The cell wall helps to maintain the cell's shape and protect its insides. It also prevents the cell from bursting. Two major groups of bacteria vary in their cell wall design. One group has a very thick **carbohydrate** layer, while the other has a thin carbohydrate layer that's covered with a second outer membrane. When stained with a violet dye, a bacterium cell with a thick wall will turn purple. A bacterium with a thin wall will not.

Bacterium Structure

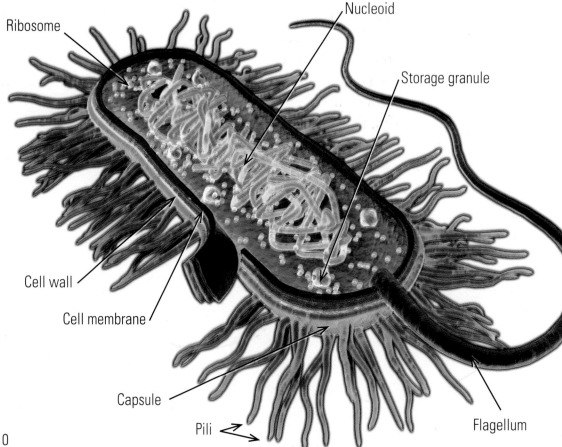

Ribosome

Nucleoid

Storage granule

Cell wall

Cell membrane

Capsule

Pili

Flagellum

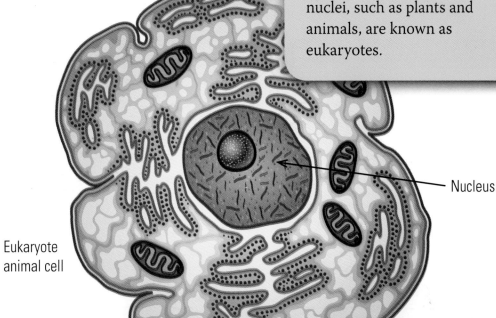

Many bacteria also have an extra outer layer called a **capsule**. This layer helps the tiny organisms stick to surfaces or to each other. In some cases, it can also protect a bacterium from being consumed by other cells.

Inside the cell membrane is the **cytoplasm**. The cytoplasm is all of a bacterium's internal parts as well as the fluid they float in. The internal parts are called **organelles**.

The **nucleoid** of a bacterium contains the cell's genetic instructions or **DNA** (deoxyribonucleic acid). This DNA is like the directions in a recipe that tell the bacterium how to eat, move, repair itself, **reproduce**, and complete all other functions. The nucleoid is tangled together, but it is not contained within its own membrane like the **nucleus** of an animal cell is.

DNA

Bacteria Are Pros

Bacteria are prokaryotes. Prokaryotes are organisms without enclosed nuclei. Life-forms with enclosed nuclei, such as plants and animals, are known as eukaryotes.

Nucleus

Eukaryote animal cell

11

Storage granules in a bacterium cell store the nutrients that the bacterium needs for energy and growth. Storage granules are like a kitchen pantry where all the ingredients for a recipe are kept until they're needed.

The "ingredients" in the storage granules are used by the **ribosomes**. Ribosomes are like chefs that follow the DNA recipes and use the ingredients in the storage granules to create **proteins**. These proteins are used to build, repair, and control the cell.

Some bacteria can form a tiny structure called an **endospore**. An endospore is a sturdy inactive form of a bacterium. These life-forms can survive in environments that kill full-grown bacteria. For example, many bacteria cannot survive when it's too hot, too cold, or too dry, but an endospore can. When conditions become favorable again, an endospore can grow into a new bacterium cell, reviving the bacteria's population.

Get Moving!

Bacteria are constantly on the move. Many bacteria have **flagella** to help them move. Flagella are long moveable "arms" that spin like propellers to move a bacterium. Other bacteria are able to move slowly by a process called *bacterial gliding*. These bacteria leave a slime trail behind them like snails do. Some bacteria don't move by themselves. Instead they rely on air or water currents to carry them.

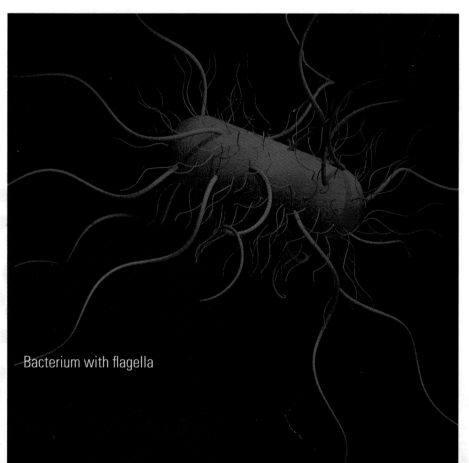

Bacterium with flagella

What's for Dinner?

When bacteria need energy, they don't just go out for a burger and fries. Some bacteria make their own food using sunlight and/or carbon dioxide. Other bacteria absorb nutrients from materials around them. Bacteria in the stomach, for instance, live off nutrients in digested food.

Binary Fission of Bacteria

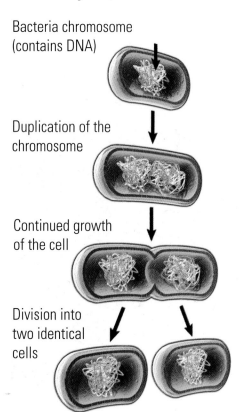

Bacteria chromosome (contains DNA)

Duplication of the chromosome

Continued growth of the cell

Division into two identical cells

Copycats

Unlike animals, which have parents that combine their DNA to create children, bacteria reproduce asexually. That means that a bacterium makes a copy of its DNA and then splits in half, creating two new bacteria with identical DNA. This process of cell division is called **binary fission**.

A new bacterium cell begins to function shortly after dividing. It is capable of reproducing again in as little as 20 minutes. In a few hours, a single bacterium can divide into millions of bacteria.

We Will Survive!

How have bacteria survived for billions of years? One reason is that bacteria can exchange **genes** with other bacteria after fission has occurred. Genes carry a cell's DNA. Bacteria can transfer genes using hairlike tubes called **pili**, which move DNA from one cell to another. These DNA transfers can pass survival characteristics present in one bacterium cell to other cells, enabling these cells to survive in situations they might not have previously been able to. For example, if a bacterium that's resistant to a medicine passes on its resistance to other bacteria, they, too, will become resistant to the medicine.

Mutation also helps bacteria multiply and survive. A mutation is a change in a cell's genes. While bacteria have the ability to repair damage to their genes, the process is not perfect and changes do occur. A few of these changes are harmful, but others are actually helpful to the bacteria. For example, suppose a bacterium has a mutation that makes it able to survive in temperatures hotter than most bacteria can tolerate. If that single bacterium survives and reproduces, it creates a whole new population of heat-resistant bacteria. This is why some species of bacteria are able to live near deep-sea volcanoes and hydrothermal vents where temperatures are extremely hot.

Hydrothermal vent

Over time, mutations help maintain and multiply bacteria populations. While each kind of bacteria has ideal conditions that allow it to thrive, mutations can help bacteria adapt to new conditions. Over time, the new conditions become the bacteria's new ideal habitat. Most bacteria thrive in warm, moist environments, but some have adapted to life in Arctic ice or hot, dry deserts. Many bacteria need oxygen to live, but others have adapted so they don't require oxygen to sustain life. Over many generations, mutations have helped bacteria survive and reproduce almost everywhere on Earth.

Tracing the Path of Science

Fossils show that bacteria known as cyanobacteria were one of the first forms of life. The oxygen released when these bacteria made food paved the way for the existence of other organisms.

It took until the mid-1600s for humans to first observe live bacteria. This was done by Anton van Leeuwenhoek, who used simple microscopes to study organisms he called *animalcules*. Many of these animalcules were later identified as bacteria.

Over the next 200 years, many scientists studied the tiny organisms. One of these men, Christian Gottfried Ehrenberg, is believed to have given them the name *bacteria*. The name came from the Greek word for "staff" (a stick or rod). Bacteria were not fully understood, however, until the invention of modern microscopes in the early 1900s.

Anton van Leeuwenhoek

chapter 3

An Overview of Viruses

Viruses are a bit trickier to classify than bacteria. Bacteria are definitely living things. They can live, grow, and reproduce on their own. Viruses, on the other hand, can only reproduce and sustain life by attaching themselves to a **host** organism. So while they can exhibit living characteristics at times, they are not true living things.

Poisonous Partner

The word *virus* comes from a Latin word that means "poison."

Sizing Up Viruses

Viruses are even smaller than bacteria. The largest virus is as small as the tiniest bacteria. More than 200 million viruses could fit on the dot over the *i* in virus. No virus is visible to the human eye. Powerful electron microscopes are necessary to see these tiny invaders.

Getting in Shape

Viruses come in a variety of shapes. Many of them are geometric figures with many sides. Others are spheres, ovals, or domes with points or spikes extending outward. A few are shaped like rounded rods or bricks.

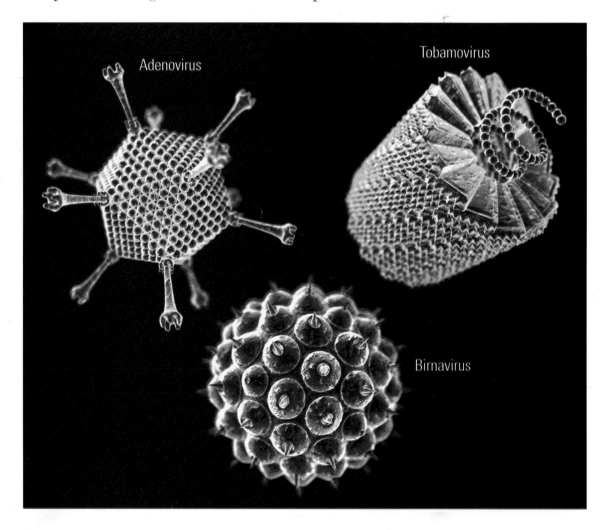

Adenovirus

Tobamovirus

Birnavirus

No Cells Here!

Viruses do not have cells. Instead they are composed of a shell containing genetic instructions. The shell is called a **capsid**. Inside the capsid are a set of genes in the form of DNA or **RNA** (ribonucleic acid). One group of RNA viruses are called *retroviruses*. Human immunodeficiency virus (HIV) is a retrovirus.

Naked Viruses

Some viruses have a third part called an **envelope**. The envelope surrounds the capsid. Viruses with an envelope are called *enveloped viruses*. Viruses without an envelope are called *naked viruses*.

Virus Structure

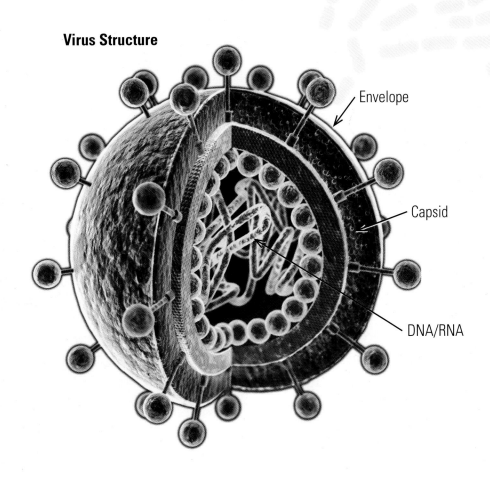

Envelope

Capsid

DNA/RNA

A Destructive Copy Machine

Although viruses can survive for a few hours on their own, they need living cells in order to reproduce. Viruses attack plant, animal, and even bacterial cells.

When a virus comes in contact with a cell, it hijacks the cell, turning it into a virus factory. How does this happen? The virus's capsid attaches itself to a host's cell wall so the virus's genes can be squirted into the cell. Once inside the cell, a virus may do different things. Some viruses live inside the cell without harming it. Others kill the cell or cause it to grow abnormally. Abnormal viral growth is what causes warts and some types of cancer. In a typical viral infection, the virus genes take over the cell's ribosomes and force them to create more copies of the virus. The cell continues to produce viruses until it explodes, spreading the viruses around. These "exploding" viruses then invade other cells and repeat the process.

Viral Attack on a Cell

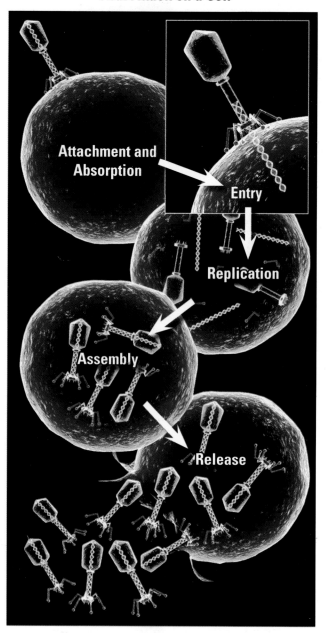

Attachment and Absorption

Entry

Replication

Assembly

Release

Volunteers wore masks to protect themselves while feeding families stricken by an influenza epidemic.

More Mutation Survivors

Viruses mutate in the same way that bacteria do. Viruses with successful mutations survive to reproduce more of themselves. The mutation rate in viruses is high because each infection creates many new viruses carrying the mutation. Some viruses mutate so much that they become dangerous to humans even though they didn't start out that way. An example of this was the Spanish flu of 1918. This deadly flu spread across the world, killing more than 50 million people. Scientists believe the flu was caused by a bird virus that mutated quickly until it was harmful to humans.

A virus's weakness is that, unlike bacteria, it has no ability to repair itself. Any damage to a virus's genes is permanent. This damage is then passed on to new viruses, causing more and more random changes. As a virus reproduces, these changes sometimes cause it to self-destruct by preventing it from infecting new cells and reproducing.

Tracing the Path of Science

Viruses didn't leave fossil evidence behind, so scientists don't know for sure when they first existed. It was in the late 1800s, however, that two scientists, Adolf Mayer and Dmitri Ivanovski, recognized the effects of viruses on tobacco plants. In 1898, Martinus Beijerinck distinguished the difference between bacteria and viruses by determining that the material damaging the tobacco plants could only reproduce in the plants, not on its own as bacteria could. He was the first to use the term *virus*.

The first human virus was discovered in 1900 when the yellow fever virus was identified. But it wasn't until the invention of the electron microscope in 1931 that the world of viruses was truly unveiled.

Electron microscope

chapter 4

Bacteria and Viruses in the Body

Most of the bacteria and viruses in your body are no threat to you. However, a few harmful bacteria and viruses sometimes manage to get past all of your defenses and attack you. How does this happen? And how can you prevent it?

How Do They Get In?

Your skin is a mighty fortress that protects you against most of the bacteria and viruses that try to invade your body. But if your skin is scraped or cut, sneaky bacteria and viruses can slip in. They can also bypass your skin's protection by hiding in food and drink that you consume or in the air that you breathe. Bacteria and viruses can even get into your eyes when you're not looking!

Your body can defend itself against most bacteria and viruses. But being on the defense all the time takes a lot of energy. If you are tired, weak, or sick, bacteria and viruses take advantage of you and move in.

Once They're In

Once bacteria get into your body, they can cause problems. Bacteria don't necessarily set out to harm you. Sometimes as bacteria go about their normal processes, their byproducts are harmful to your body. For example, your teeth develop cavities because the *Lactobacillus acidophilus* bacteria that live in your mouth break down sugars. When they do this, the bacteria create an acid as a byproduct.

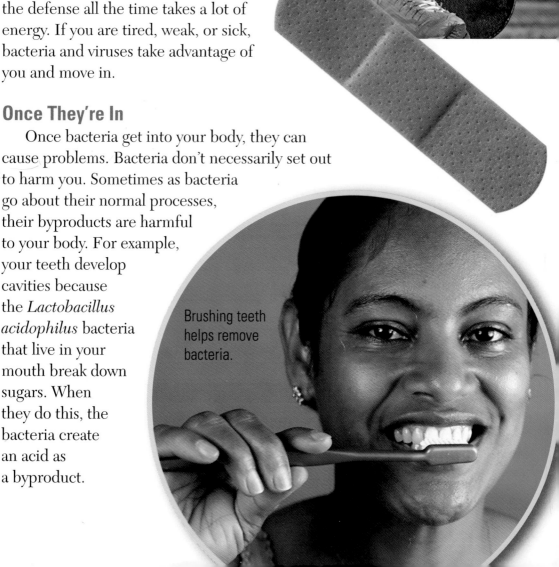

Brushing teeth helps remove bacteria.

That acid just happens to dissolve the hard coating on your teeth, making way for a cavity. Other times, bacteria actually consume healthy cells in your body. When you're infected with salmonella bacteria, for example, the bacteria cells feed on the cells in your intestines, causing painful stomach problems.

When a virus enters your body, it searches for a cell to infect. A cold or flu virus will look for cells in your lungs or stomach. A human immunodeficiency virus will head toward white blood cells that fight off infections. Once a virus locates the "right" cell, it takes over its normal functions to create more viruses. When cells can't proceed with their regular jobs, your body is threatened.

Heading Off Intruders

There are simple things you can do to prevent bacteria and viruses from entering your body. Washing your hands before eating and after using the bathroom stops the transfer of **germs**. Cleaning wounds with antibacterial products and covering them with a bandage forms a seal on injured skin. Not eating raw eggs, undercooked poultry, unwashed fruits and vegetables, or foods that haven't been refrigerated properly keeps bacteria out of your stomach. Staying away from people who already have an infection keeps you from getting their germs.

People, such as doctors, dentists, and daycare workers, who regularly come in contact with other people's wounds, blood, or germs, wear masks and gloves to protect both themselves and the people they work with from the spread of bacteria and viruses. Tools, toys, dishes, and other items that are reused by many people should be disinfected to prevent the "sharing" of germs.

Inquire and Investigate
Antibacterial Products

Question

What effect do antibacterial products have on bacteria reproduction?

Answer the Question

I think that antibacterial products _____

_____.

Form a Hypothesis

Antibacterial products _____ bacteria growth.

Test the Hypothesis

Materials

package of agar (gel used to grow microscopic organism)

2 petri dishes with covers

refrigerator

1 sheet of blotter paper

permanent marker

4 different antibacterial products in a liquid form (Lysol, bleach, alcohol, antibacterial soap, etc.)

tap water

tweezers

Procedure

▷ Prepare 30 ml of the agar according to the directions. Pour enough of the solution into two petri dishes so the bottoms are covered. Cover the dishes immediately and let them stand until the agar is firm. Refrigerate the petri dishes upside down until you're ready to begin the experiment.

▷ Take the petri dishes out of the refrigerator and leave them upright with the covers off for about an hour.

▷ While bacteria are gathering in the dishes, cut five 5-mm squares of blotter paper. Label four of them with the initials of the antibacterial products you're testing. Label the fifth square H_2O. This one will test water as your experiment control. (Water does not contain any antibacterial products.)

▷ Soak the labeled squares in the matching product and wipe off any excess. Use the tweezers to place the squares in one of the petri dishes. Make sure the squares aren't touching and are spread apart as much as possible.

▷ Let the second petri dish sit undisturbed. This is your control, which will show normal bacterial growth.

▷ Cover the petri dishes and place them in a dark place for five days. Then retrieve the dishes and observe the bacteria growth in each one.

Observations

The control dish should demonstrate the most bacteria growth. The squares with the antibacterial products in it should show stunted or no growth. (The rate of growth will vary among products.) The square with water on it should be similar to the control dish.

Conclusions

Antibacterial products slow or stop bacteria growth. Some products are more effective than others at stopping the spread of bacteria.

When all precautions fail and a bacterium or virus does invade your body, your **immune system** steps in. Your immune system is an internal security system. It constantly scans your body looking for things that don't belong. When it finds them, it takes action to get rid of them. For example, when the common cold, or rhinovirus, infects you, your immune system fights back. A runny nose is your immune system trying to flush the virus out your nose. The stuff you cough up is another attempt to get rid of the virus. A fever is also a sign that your immune system is at work. Hotter temperatures make it more difficult for bacteria and viruses to survive.

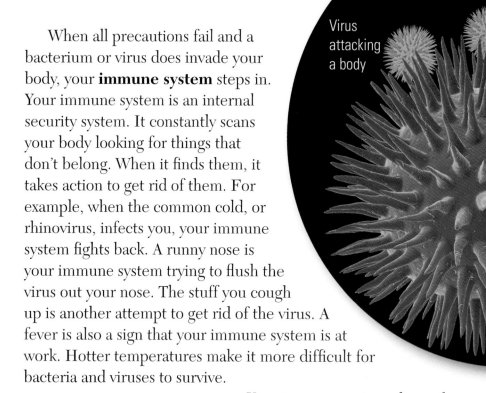

Virus attacking a body

Your immune system also makes custom-designed proteins to stop viruses and bacteria. These substances are called **antibodies**. Some of these antibodies stay in your body even after the bacteria or virus is gone to make sure that it doesn't return. That's why once you get the chicken pox, you'll likely never get it again.

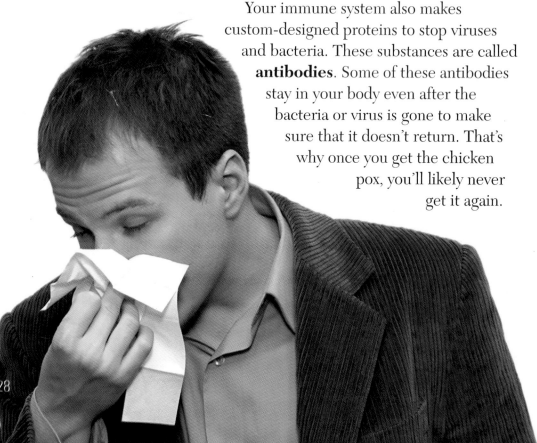

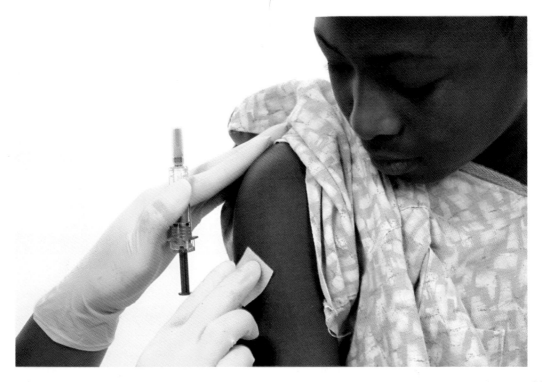

Scientists have figured out how to use your immune system to destroy bacteria and viruses before they attack. Scientists take a bacteria or virus and alter it so it isn't as harmful to your body. The weakened material, called a **vaccine**, is injected into your body. This is known as **immunization**. When your immune system spots the vaccine invader, it creates antibodies to destroy it. Now if the original form of the bacteria or virus enters your body, your body already has the necessary antibodies to protect against it. You probably received many immunizations before going to school to fight off invaders such as the measles virus and the pneumococcal bacteria that can cause pneumonia.

Scientist of Significance

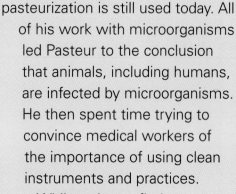

Louis Pasteur (1822–1895) was a French chemist and microbiologist. He was an early supporter of the germ theory of disease, which states that diseases are caused by **microbes** such as bacteria and viruses.

Through his experiments, Pasteur figured out that **fermentation** is caused by the growth of microorganisms. He also found that heating milk kills any bacteria and molds in it. This process of milk pasteurization is still used today. All of his work with microorganisms led Pasteur to the conclusion that animals, including humans, are infected by microorganisms. He then spent time trying to convince medical workers of the importance of using clean instruments and practices.

While trying to find a cure for chicken cholera, Pasteur accidentally created a weakened version of the disease. He discovered that animals infected with a weakened version of a disease become immune to the original disease. This was the basis for modern immunization.

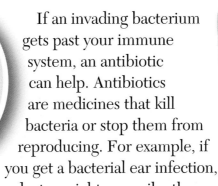

If an invading bacterium gets past your immune system, an antibiotic can help. Antibiotics are medicines that kill bacteria or stop them from reproducing. For example, if you get a bacterial ear infection, your doctor might prescribe the antibiotic amoxicillin to treat it. Unfortunately, the overuse of antibiotics has resulted in some bacteria becoming resistant to them so they're no longer an effective treatment.

Viruses, on the other hand, cannot be treated with antibiotics. Medicines can be used to lessen symptoms of an infection such as coughing or a runny nose, but they don't destroy the virus. A person with a virus has to wait it out until the immune system successfully eliminates the virus.

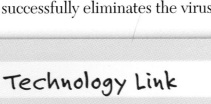

Technology Link

Penicillin was one of the earliest antibiotics used to treat bacterial infections. Two early scientists, Ernest Duchesne and Alexander Fleming, recognized that a mold called *Penicillium notatum* could kill other bacteria. But it wasn't until 1939 that Dr. Howard Florey and Ernst Chain isolated the bacteria-killing substance found in the mold and proved that it could be used to kill harmful bacteria in humans. The scientists then worked to produce large quantities of the antibiotic. Luckily, this was accomplished in time to treat injured soldiers in World War II. Before penicillin, infected wounds were the biggest cause of death in soldiers. Today penicillin is used to treat many bacterial infections, including strep throat, pneumonia, bronchitis, and tetanus.

chapter 5

Not Always the Bad Guys

The world is full of bacteria and viruses. However, only a small percent of bacteria are harmful to humans. And in fact, many bacteria are actually helpful. Even viruses can be the good guys once in a while.

Bacteria in the Body

Much of the bacteria in the human body plays an important role. Bacteria help in the production and absorption of nutrients such as magnesium and vitamins B and K. Bacteria in the intestines help digest food. Helpful bacteria also keep "bad" bacteria under control by using up resources and crowding them out.

Bacteria can be used to make medicines that treat infections in the body. Many of the antibiotics prescribed for bacterial infections are actually made from bacteria. Genetically altered bacteria are used to create insulin for diabetics.

Eating Bacteria

Many of the foods you enjoy exist thanks to bacteria. Bacteria are used to make dairy products such as cheese, yogurt, and sour cream. Bacteria are responsible for the "sour" in sourdough bread. The vinegar used to pickle vegetables and fish is made from bacteria. Coffee, chocolate, and sausage all depend on bacteria for their production.

Backyard Bacteria

Bacteria keep dead things from piling up around you. Bacteria break down, or decompose, dead plants and animals and return nutrients to the soil to help new plants grow.

Bacteria help plants in another way too. Bacteria in the soil and living on plants convert nitrogen in the air and soil into materials that plants need for growth.

Bacteria Power

When bacteria that live in wetlands decompose materials in their environment, they produce methane gas. Methane is a natural gas that can be used for cooking and heating. Scientists have also created a bacterium that can turn corn and other plants into a type of alcohol called *ethanol*. Ethanol is a high-quality fuel additive that burns cleanly in cars.

Bacterial Clean-Up

Some bacteria "eat" oil or poisons in toxic waste. These bacteria can be used to clean up oil spills or landfills because they consume and break down dangerous materials.

Dr. Anada Chakrabarty created an oil-eating bacteria that can be used to clean up oil spills. The Supreme Court upheld his patent on the bacteria. It was the first patent ever granted to a life-form made in a lab.

Go Viruses!

A virus's ability to infect cells is a powerful tool in medicine and research. Scientists can remove and replace the genes in certain viruses. A modified virus can then be injected into diseased cells in a body. When the virus takes over the cells, it spreads the repaired genes. This is called *gene therapy*.

Viruses are also being used to fight cancer. Modified viruses can be injected into cancer cells to shut them down.

Bacteria and viruses often get a bad rap because they can make you sick. But it's important to remember the benefits of having bacteria and viruses around.

http://www.microbe.org/

Solve the mysteries of bacteria and viruses with the information, news, and experiments at this fun site.

http://www.geocities.com/bacterial_ed/intro.htm

If you're a beginner at bacteria, this is the place to start. Find out how bacteria affects foods, industries, nature, and other areas of life.

http://commtechlab.msu.edu/sites/dlc–me/zoo/

Visit the Microbe Zoo to learn more about bacteria and viruses.

http://microbeworld.org/htm/aboutmicro/ microbes/types_start.htm

Get the basics on bacteria and viruses, and check out the "Bacteria/Viruses of Note."

http://cellsalive.com/cells/bactcell. htm

Interact with a bacterium cell diagram. Then go to the bacteria cell cam to watch streptococcus pneumoniae cells, the bacteria that cause pneumonia, reproduce.

http://www.smm.org/tissues/

This "Tissues of Life" site includes a game about bacterial and viral invaders as well as a chance to "meet" a virologist.

antibiotic (ant eye beye AH tik) medicine used to kill bacteria or stop their reproduction

antibody (ANT uh bah dee) protein that fights against harmful bacteria or viruses in a body

bacteria (bak TEAR ee uh) single-celled organism without a nucleus

binary fission (BEYE nair ee FISH uhn) division of a single-celled organism into two identical cells

capsid (KAP sid) outer coat of protein that surrounds a virus

capsule (KAP suhl) outer layer on some bacteria that helps them stick to surfaces

carbohydrate (kar boh HEYE drayt) material made from carbon, hydrogen, and oxygen

cell membrane (sel MEM brayn) thin, flexible band around a cell that controls the movement of substances in and out of the cell

cell wall (sel wawl) outer layer of a bacterium that provides shape, support, and protection

cytoplasm (SEYE tuh plaz uhm) all of the living material inside a bacteria cell

DNA (dee en ay) molecule that contains genetic information for making proteins; deoxyribonucleic acid

endospore (END oh spor) small, thick-coated, resistant form of a bacterium

envelope (EN vuh lohp) outer membrane layer on the outside of some viruses that helps a virus enter host cells

37

fermentation (fer men TAY shuhn) process by which a microorganism breaks down a substance into simpler ones without the presence of oxygen, such as in the use of yeast to break down sugars to produce alcohol

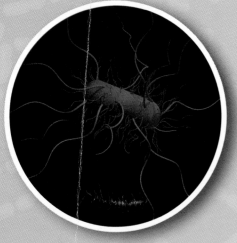

flagella (fluh JEL uh) skinny whiplike outgrowths on a bacterium cell used for motion

gene (jeen) segment of DNA that contains information for making a particular protein

germ (jerm) tiny organism or particle, such as a bacterium or virus, that causes disease

host (hohst) organism in or on which another organism or a virus lives

immune system (uh MYOUN SIS tuhm) a body's system of recognizing and fighting foreign substances in the body

immunization (im you nuh ZAY shuhn) using a vaccine to protect against bacterial and viral infections

microbe (MEYE krohb) tiny body, such as a bacterium or virus, that can only be seen under a microscope

nucleoid (NOO klee oyd) cluster of DNA in a bacterium cell

nucleus (NOO klee uhs) DNA-containing organelle that controls an animal cell's activities

organelle (OR guh nel) small structure inside a cell that carries out certain jobs

pili (PEYE leye) hairlike tubes that transfer DNA between bacteria

protein (PROH teen) large molecule found in all cells that helps with the growth, repair, and replacement of cells

reproduce (ree pruh DOOS) to make more of a living thing

ribosome (REYE buh sohm) organelle that makes proteins

RNA (ar en ay) molecule that is key in making proteins; ribonucleic acid

storage granule (STOR uhj GRAN youl) cluster of stored nutrients in a bacterium

vaccine (vak SEEN) medicine made of a weakened, dead, or broken up bacteria or virus that triggers the production of antibodies for protection

virus (VEYE ruhs) tiny particle that infects and reproduces inside the cells of organisms